From My Mind

Emily Borgia

BookLeaf Publishing

India | USA | UK

Presentation by *BookLeaf Publishing*

Web: www.bookleafpub.com

E-mail: info@bookleafpub.com

ISBN: 978-93-5744-996-0

First edition 2022

DEDICATION

To my nan, the strongest woman I have known.

You were battling so much more than you let anyone know.

We all miss you so much.

PREFACE

As a person who has battled with mental health her whole life, this is a collection of my own thoughts, feelings and experiences with my own anxieties. It also discusses topics of loss, abuse and the occasional lighthearted moment of happiness to spruce it up. But it really does come from my head and my heart.
Please remember to always be kind.

In My Head

In my head there are a thousand tabs open
Like a computer screen
Not neatly assorted
Scattered, fighting for space
A train collision
Where everything is on fire
The tracks all merge
And I cant make sense of why

In my head I am stupid
Too loud and not loud enough
I sit alone with people there
But I don't compare
To the way they look or think
I am smiling
But truely on the brink
Because today I cant manage
To even say Hi

In my head I need to move
All the time
Like literally all the time
Move my fingers and toes
I need to scratch my nose
And find a way

For my thoughts to stay thoughts
And not fidget
I really need to try

In my head I hear everything
The alarm
Chewing
Just make it stop
I know what Susan is buying
Or why Paul cant go home
I want some quiet
I want to be alone
All these sounds
And I just want to cry

In my head the world never stops
My brain never sleeps
Like an energiser bunny
'Just rest'
Now thats funny
Because I don't ever rest
Not for a second
When my eyes close
The my world comes to life
If I could just have a minute
To tell everything in my head
GOODBYE

A Good Day

Today was a good day
At least i think it was
Today was, what you'd call
'A fine day'

But remember when you tried to say...
But instead it came out as...
And then they couldn't even look your way
Now thats not was I call a 'fine day'

Oh I remember
How could I forgot
Why would I say it that way
Now i'll live with regret

Its burned in my memory
Oh look they want to say 'hey'
Don't answer
Just turn and walk away

No no today was fine, it was particularly okay
Although remember when you tried to say...

Oh, today was a bad day
Today was a very bad day
Indeed.

Musical Mask

She rocks, sadly in the corner of the house
Unable to walk, or speak
The anxiety has made her world so bleak
And yet she decides she must go on

Each day further and further
First the front door, the mailbox,
Then the corner store
Each day she gets up and tries

And she continues to cry
But nobody sees her
Her true self hides
Behind her beautiful musical mask

The singing never has words
But contains so many feelings
And yet so often she sings
But continues to be unheard

20 years of battle
And fight and struggle
Against her own relentless mind
And she leaves her family behind

Yet we remember the happy
The kitchen singing
We forget all her struggles
As we enter a new beginning

For now she is gone
Her body and her mind
Yet her true self left years ago
When the anxiety robbed her blind

Friendship

Rose are red
Violets are blue
Inside I bleed
Just like you do

We may look different
But I don't care
Because you are kind
And offer to share

You share with me your world
Through thick and thin
To have you as a friend
Is truly a big win

For life is uncertain
And scary and unkind
But I will make it through
With you by my side

Because lavender is purple
And lilies smell nice
A brunette and a blondie,
our friendship is my vice

The Rain

I love the way the rain falls
So unapologetically
Its loud and messy and comes whenever it likes
It commands attention
Its presence cannot be overlooked
You cannot overlook the rain
Some people love the rain
And others definitely don't
Some wish its presence was smaller
Less significant, quieter
While others dance with the rain
Splash in all its glory
Celebrate the rain
The rain makes people comfortable
And familiar
While others haven't seen the rain in years
Years without the rains commanding presence
A drought, an absence
Of the wonderful, beautiful, loud, messy rain

Dear Daughter

Dear daughter,
The world is an overwhelmingly scary place
Filled with hate and violence and diseases
I have thought about not brining you into such a
world
But I cannot wait to meet you
To celebrate you
I want to hold you in my arms and keep you my
baby forever
But soon you will learn that my love cannot
protect you
It cannot save you
You will see the hate, the violence and disease
You will still be taught girls aren't as smart
Or as strong
Or as significant as men
But you are
We are!
As women we care so deeply
We overanalyse everything
And we are smart, and strong and significant
And you can do and be whatever you want
I will be here for the hurt
All the tears

And I will teach you to be everything a woman
can be
And I will show you your body is your own
That no man can take your body from you
I will teach you beauty is on the inside
Empathy, passion, courage
Is beauty!
So I don't have all the answers
I am still learning too
And god help me for trying to raise a daughter
With as much fire and sass as me
But Dear Daughter,
We are a team.
You and I
We will conquer this world
And we will teach each other things
We are strong and beautiful and smart and kind
We are women
And dear daughter
I cannot wait to meet you.

Heroes

I decided to become a nurse one day
Just woke up and went 'hey'
This is my new life
I woke up and committed myself to a new world
A world I thought was about empathy
With likeminded people
Boy was I wrong
Because while nursing isn't about money
And it's not without its share of C**P
It certainly feels like
You've entered a trap
I met people who didn't seem to care
Who literally acted like their patients aren't
there
I have met others with a heart of gold
Who struggle to understand what we are told
About how the hospital works
With its politics and ladders
Because trust me when I tell you nurses don't
matter
We bust our bodies, our hearts and our minds
To try to get a glimpse of hope
From our patients' weary eyes
Then we entered a pandemic
The heroes they call us

With our bruised faces from masks
We want it to be anyone but us
We are frightened to come
To see our loved ones face
Because we are tired and angry
And don't want them ashamed
Of the people we have become
We have lost all hope
Because the world we once entered
The shift work, the patient care
Has become a sad and scary world
And I don't want to work there

Puberty

Your hair grows longer
Then it appears
Your legs and armpits
Shaving is tackling a fear

Girl you've got hips
Growing from east to west
You've now got to fit them in jeans
So just do your best

Try running with boobs
Its really a task!
You poke and prod the girls
To fit them in an uncomfortable bra

Now once a month becomes quite tricky
As you navigate your feelings
Believe me in certain situations
You've got to act quickly

They call this phase puberty
Its when you grow up
And I'm not going to lie
Girl it really sucks

Permanently Exhausted Pigeon

I have never felt more seen than when one says
I am not a night owl or early bird
But one permanently exhausted pigeon
I have found this to always be true
I wake up tired
I spend the entire day tired
Sometimes I'm exhausted just to mix it up
And then at night time
You guess it, still tired.
And perhaps its because my brain never sleeps
Or as humans we are devolving
We no longer have prey
So we can sleep as long as we like
We spend all our time at rapid speed
That our body no longer copes
I am tired
Of always working fast
Walking fast
Thinking fast
And if you hesitate for a minute
You are considered slow

And you don't want to be slow
So we are fast
And tired
And fast again
Forever

Not Just a Dog

When I look into their eyes,
I feel like their world
They see me for who I am
They depend on me
For everything
Yet they think I'm amazing
They think I am god damn amazing
You see, animals are honest
Their big brown eyes tell everything
They know who is genuine
Who can p**s off
And who needs some extra love
They can tell when you're sick
Or when you're hurting
And they are just your best little friend
Why would you not have a pet
A best friend
A fur baby
Or whoever they are to you
Because at the end of the day
We all deserve to feel amazing
In someone's little eyes

Not. My. Fault.

You lose feeling when it happens
Like your body goes numb
Your mind goes elsewhere
You submit
He strokes your hair
Before pulling it. Hard.
His hand round my neck
I cant breathe
But without that
I still couldn't scream
I felt like I deserved it
His body on mine
His weight pushing me down
I went on the date
So you can shut up and take it
Or so I thought anyway
It wasn't just rough sex
It wasn't sex at all
I still feel that night
I still go back to that night
In my head
And in my body
Like I just want to curl up and cry
He took the one thing from me
I feel like I can never get back

Sex. Actual sex.
I still feel him breathing down my neck
Pulling my hair
And I don't know if that feeling will ever leave
I never thought I would be silly enough
Stupid enough
To be in that position
But it was never my fault
And it will never. Ever. Be my fault.

The Worst Show

I feel like I'm watching my life happen
A spectator to a sometimes-terrible show
Like I get no say in the course
The outcome
I don't even have a program to the show
There's often weird music playing
I'm singing even if I don't know the words
And nothing makes sense at all
I want everything to stop
Freeze
Or just even bloody slow down
So I can take a minute to breathe
And to really take in what is happening
If anyone is buying tickets
I do not recommend
I am leaving very poor reviews
Characters have died, got sick or left
There is stress and angst and rage
Fortunately, there is a love story
Everyone loves a love story
And a fairy-tale wedding
So why not try your luck
Watch the show and help me out
Make me the hero will you
Because I need a good show

You're Asking For It

You have a drink
You're asking for it
You wear that dress you love
You're asking for it
Oh you went on a date
You must have been asking for it
Made the effort to dress nice
Asking for it
Thought about it and changed your mind
Definitely asking for it
Said no
Oh but you don't really mean that
You must still be asking for it
You're a girl
By default you're asking for it

Crazy

They call us crazy
Those whose minds work differently
Work faster or slower
Or possess the ability to change rapidly
Those who can reach a place so dark no one can
see
Or like me
Can create a scenario so left field no one
understands
Those who needs medication
Or have found a friend in psychology
We are crazy
Crazy talented
Crazy smart
Crazy creative
Crazy strong
Crazy unique
And our minds are crazy beautiful
So call me crazy
I can follow crazy with many adjectives
I can be all kinds of crazy
And so can you

The More You Know

Knowledge is power
It allows you the ability to say you're wrong
But are they wrong?
If it is factual, then probably
But if it can be viewed differently
No, they're not wrong
I think knowledge allows you the power to teach
To pass on the knowledge
To explain the why
Not just the what
Knowledge impacts the future
Because ignorance will hold us back
From developing
Moving on
Growing
But the most important thing to do with power
Is to elevate others
So teach
Educate
Encourage
And some day we may all have the power
Of knowledge

My Husband

I promised you me
Every bit of me
I committed myself to you
Because since the first day I met you
And every day since
I have loved you
I love your soul
And your passion
My best friend
And we fight
Oh boy do we fight
But love is about passion
With passion you fight
But I am always right
Together forever
Bound by our love
And our rings
Our next adventure begins
A house and children
In a whole new city
But for a good reason
I would follow you anywhere
As you have followed me
From city to the sea

Let's enjoy our next chapter
Whatever that will be.

Am I an Introvert?

An introvert I thought
As I lost friends
I wondered why they left
But they must leave
To make space in my life
For the next group of people
Too many people
I'm overwhelmed
So, I keep my circle close
Too close
I open up again
For I can keep friends
Some have never gone
Here all along
Through the good and the bad
When I've been particularly mad
And their company I do enjoy
Maybe an extrovert at times
I could always give it a try

Country Love

The country is where I'd rather be
The silence, the silage, the trees
Where you neighbour is a long way down the
road
And everyone works in a go-slow mode
People stop to say Hello
And yes, your business everyone knows
The country roads where you hit a Roo
And they do more damage than people do
You have to travel to get anywhere
But the corner store, everyone gathers there
The rolling hills and the water stream
Seem to bleak when the fire alarm screams
We've been through it all
Flood, fire and drought
But the country spirit is strong
And it'll live on, I have no doubt